WELCOME TO THE GOOD LIFE

David S. Philemon

Royal Diadem Publishing Inc.

Dedication

To the Almighty God, my foundation and ever-present help. I am grateful for Your boundless love and grace that sustain me daily. And to my mentor in ministry, Rev. George Izunwa, whose steadfast commitment to the call of God has deeply impacted my life. Your guidance and support have been invaluable, encouraging me to walk boldly in the path God has set before me. Thank you for your example and your heart for the Kingdom.

ACKNOWLEDGMENT

This book would not have been possible without the unwavering support, dedication, and talent of an extraordinary team. My deepest gratitude goes to each of you for your contributions, insights, and encouragement throughout this journey.

First and foremost, thank you to Rev. Mimi Philemon my dear wife, Rev. Shina Gentry, and and my assistant pastor Rev. Bright Amudoaghan for your incredible effort, encouragement, and belief in this project. Your support has been instrumental in bringing this vision to life.

To the dedicated leaders of Royal Diadem Publishing, Ide Imogie and Kishawna Bailey, I am immensely grateful for your belief in this project from the very beginning and for investing your time and energy into its development. Your creativity, dedication, and expertise have been the backbone of this endeavor.

I am especially grateful to the Royal Diadem Publishing team— Beulah Orogun, Emmanuella Ben-Eboh, Doyinsade Awodele, Kim Matthews, and Shante Gill, for your meticulous attention to detail, refining every page and ensuring that each word reflects our vision.

A heartfelt thank you to my family, friends, and colleagues whose unwavering support and belief in this project gave me the courage and strength to see it through.

Finally, thank you to all the readers and supporters who make this work meaningful. I am humbled and honored to share this journey with each of you.

With all my gratitude,
David Philemon

CONTENTS

INTRODUCTION

I have often met people going through great trials and situations that leave them in tears, filled with sorrow, and burdened by a heavy heart. Many cry and wish for a better life, hoping for a day when things will finally turn around. Sometimes they ask, "Why me? Why does life seem so full of pain and sadness?" The truth is, we have all experienced these moments at some point in our lives. But let me tell you, this is not what God wants for you. God never intended for your life to be defined by tears, pain, or sorrow. His plan has always been that you live a life of joy, glory, protection, health, abundance, fulfillment, and more. In other words, His desire for you has always been the good life.

This book, *"Welcome to the Good Life"* is a revelation from the throne of heaven, and it is designed to open your eyes to the path that leads to the life God has always intended for you. This is not just about fleeting happiness or temporary relief from your struggles. It is about stepping into a life of lasting peace, joy, abundance, and more. You see, the good life is not just something to wish for, it's something God has already made available to you.

Many people mistakenly believe that God wants them to remain in hardship and that maybe their trials are a sign that He has forgotten them. But Jeremiah 29:11 says, *"For I know the thoughts that I think toward you, saith the Lord, thoughts of peace, and not of evil, to give you an expected end."* Can you see this revelation which shows that God's intention is not for you to stay in pain or to live in sorrow? He desires to give you hope, to lead you into a future where your tears are wiped away, and where you experience the fullness of His blessings.

But here's something important: although God's desire for you is to live the good life, there is a requirement- you cannot simply wish your way into it or expect to step into it without any effort on your part. God is not a *genie* who grants wishes just at the snap of your fingers. If you are truly serious about living the good life, the life that God has for you, then you must be willing to cooperate with Him. There is a partnership involved in experiencing the life God has planned for you.

One of the greatest misunderstandings many believers have is that they think God will do everything while they do absolutely nothing. Well, it's time to wake up and realize that just as you are counting on God, God is also counting on you to play your part. As a matter of fact, we can always trust God to play His role; the problem often resides with us.

This book is not just any book; it's a revelation of all that you need to effectively cooperate with God. You did not pick it by mistake or by luck; it's God Himself who has brought this book your way because He wants to bring you into the Good life and He has been longing for your cooperation.

Don't just read it as though you are reading a novel, realize that God is about to flood your heart with revelation. And He expects that as He does so, you will cooperate with Him in full obedience so that, through you and the good life He brings you into, men will give glory to your Father which is in Heaven.

Child of God, it's a new season for you!

Welcome to the Good Life!

CHAPTER ONE

THE MYSTERY OF PROGRESS AND DIVINE GUIDANCE

"Any step forward that pulls you away from God is not progress, but a trap.

The Path Of True Progress

B y the mighty power of Jehovah, I declare unto you that as you read today, God Almighty shall transition you into a new realm of mysterious rest. Now, before we start moving into the deep things of the spirit and exploring "the Good Life," it is imperative that you, first of all, lay hold on the true meaning of progress because it is God's divine intention for each one of us as His children to continually progress in life.

So, what exactly is progress? In very basic terms, to make progress means you are moving higher, you are moving further and you are an achiever. However, in our present-day society, it is quite unfortunate that some seek to redefine the word *progress* in a manner that is quite demonic. Although being progressive is indeed God's will for us, these misguided people are attempting to portray it as though being progressive means abandoning all that is good and righteous in favor of mundane and utter foolishness. The way they present it nowadays, one might think that being progressive is the same as embracing stupidity, but let me assure you, our God Almighty is a God of progress.

Read this carefully. I need to lay the foundation very firmly here before we go further. Know this and never forget it: any so-called progress that draws you away from God is not progress but a trap, that is not true progress at all! Let me say it again: any achievement, no matter how great it may seem, that weakens your relationship with the Lord is destructive, therefore, do not deceive yourself into believing you are making progress simply because you are accumulating material possessions or experiencing fleeting moments of worldly pleasure. The Word of God warns us in Proverbs 14:12 (KJV) saying, *"There is a way which seemeth right unto a man, but the end thereof are the ways of death."* When you find yourself making progress in the wrong direction, know that you are headed straight for destruction, and, mark my words, you shall eventually pay a heavy price for your misguided steps. But you may ask, *How can one discern whether they are progressing in the right direction?* The answer, my friends, is simple: the right direction will always draw you closer to God, while the wrong direction will pull you away.

The right path helps you honor God in the manner He desires to be honored, not in the way you presume to honor Him because true progress always takes into account God's divine agenda and the welfare of His people. This is precisely why it is of utmost importance to hear God's voice in all matters of life. As it is written in Hosea 12:13 (KJV), *"And by a prophet the Lord brought Israel out of Egypt, and by a prophet was he preserved."* This is a revelation that coming out of a dire situation of circumstance is glorious, but then, merely coming out is never enough, being preserved is the key to true progress.

Let us examine the example of the Israelites. They were indeed brought out of Egypt, but if you study the book of Deuteronomy, you will find that they wandered in the wilderness for 39 years, not 40 as commonly believed. The 40th year was their exit from the wilderness. Why, you may wonder, did it take so long? It was because that was the time required for God to purge those who murmured against Him.

God spoke to Moses, declaring that those rebellious souls would perish in the wilderness, and Moses, as any good leader would do, decided to intercede on their behalf, and God in His infinite mercy heard his plea. Yet, those with stubborn hearts were still denied entry into the land of rest because God couldn't afford to allow them to enter into the land with such a spirit of stubbornness and lack of faith in Him. This is because even in the promised land of rest, there are temptations and trials to be faced. Can you imagine the catastrophe that would have ensued had they carried their rebellion into the land? Utter destruction would have followed.

This is why I always pray, *"Lord, reveal Yourself to my sons and daughters, that they may not be counted among those who perish on the other side."* As parents, our heart's desire is always for our children to partake in the mighty works of God. However, the ultimate truth is that every child must make their own decision. Take Esau, for example. He made his choice, and Jacob made his also, and they both had different results.

When God issues clear instructions, it is for our benefit and clarity. He presents us with choices, but He will not choose for us. Rather, what He does is that He advises us to choose the right path. But if we receive the blessings of God without choosing God Himself, those very blessings will soon become toxic in our lives.

I am saying this to let you know that if you truly want to experience the good life, then you must first understand what true progress means and realize that it must draw you to God, and then you must also realize that you must always prioritize and choose God over and beyond all blessings that you can get from

Him. This is the simple reason many people have not seen steady progress in their lives, and without steady progress in your life, you will never be able to truly enter the good life.

Guilt, Stubbornness, And The Journey To Promise

Right now, I am going to say some truths that may be difficult to hear, yet it is of utmost importance. You need to know that when the blessings of God fall upon a person whose heart is crooked or filled with wickedness, those very blessings become a dangerous tool in their hands. This is because blessings have the power to amplify everything within a person, be it good or evil. And when a blessing amplifies the darkness within a crooked soul, that individual will inevitably turn their amplified life against the very God who bestowed those blessings upon them. This is the reason so many people who are blessed seem to be very proud. It's not the blessings that made them proud; the blessings only amplified the pride that has always been in their heart. If it's wickedness that is resident in their heart, then the blessings will only increase.

I know you may want to say, *"But I'm different! Surely this doesn't apply to me!"* But sadly, this is how it has always been since the beginning of time, and you cannot change this fundamental truth. The wisest course of action, if you truly desire to bask in the fullness of God's blessings, is to choose God before you even consider choosing the blessing. Hence, you must make Matthew 6:33 (KJV) one of the most important guidelines of your life: *"But seek ye first the kingdom of God, and his righteousness; and all these things shall be added unto you."*

For the Israelites whom God delivered from the bondage of Egypt, the Lord's anger burned against them for their constant rebellion and lack of faith, and as a result, He decreed that they would wander in the wilderness for 40 long years. Numbers 32:13 (MSG) says, *"God's anger smoked against Israel. He made them wander in the wilderness for forty years until that entire generation that acted* out evil in his sight had died out." This was not an arbitrary punishment, but a divine plan to ensure that the entire generation that had acted wickedly in His sight would pass away before their descendants could enter the Promised Land. And here you are, standing on the precipice of your own promised land, maybe just one month away from stepping into the answers to your prayers. So, you must search your heart, and make sure your heart is right and in faith, else the same disaster which befell that generation of Israel would become your portion. But I declare that you will step into your promised land in the mighty name of Jesus.

Deuteronomy 2:14 in the KJV says, *"And the space in which we came from Kadeshbarnea, until we were come over the brook Zered, was thirty and eight years; until all the generation of the men of war were wasted out from among the host, as the Lord sware unto them."* Now read it in the MSG translation, *"We traveled from Kadesh Barnea until we crossed the Zered Brook. That took thirty-eight years. All the time, the men of war had died off, just as God had promised them."* Can you see the consequences of being wicked and not being aligned with God? Wickedness here doesn't necessarily mean murder or that you committed sin; rebellion, disobedience, murmuring against God, doubting his faithfulness, etc. are all wickedness.

I believe with all my heart that there is indeed a land flowing with milk and honey, and our gracious God is eagerly waiting for us to enter into it. Do you understand the gravity of this truth? But let me ask you: do you truly believe that God will allow just anyone to enter this promised land? God waited thirty-eight long years to bring them to the promised land. But, I believe that if they had changed during that period and said, *'Lord, we repent,'* the story would have been different today. In those 38 years, it was as though God was giving room for at least one person among them to say, *"You know what? I've had a change of heart. I repent of my stubborn ways."* This, my friends, is why you cannot lay blame at God's feet when you see someone who has been serving Him for years fail to reflect His glory. More often than not, the issue lies in the very contents of their soul, not in their outward actions. The moment you make up your mind and declare, "*God, right here and now, I receive deliverance in the depths of my soul, and I commit to walking with You progressively,*" I assure you, God will be overjoyed and from that very instant, He will begin His transformative work within you. Abraham is a prime example. God called him, but for years, did not speak to him because Lot was in his company. Yet, despite this silence, God blessed them materially. *Why?* you may ask. It's because God knew the true state of Lot's soul.

Abraham, in his human wisdom, thought he could outsmart God. He probably thought, "*This is my nephew; I cannot abandon him.*" Abraham felt a sense of responsibility towards Lot because his father, like Abraham, had attempted to serve God, but when Nimrod cast them into the flames, Lot's father was consumed, while Abraham came back alive. This was the root of Abraham's guilt. However, I implore you not to allow guilt to be the guiding force in your life. It is natural to feel responsible for others, but guilt should never be your primary motivation because there are aspects of people's lives and characters that are hidden from your eyes, but God sees all. At times, God desires to deliver you from certain individuals and, sometimes, from yourself. If there is crookedness within you, you may not be aware of it initially, but eventually, it will manifest in your actions and in the way you view the world around you.

Can you imagine this? The Israelites spent 38 years wandering in the wilderness, waiting for death to claim them. But, instead of resigning themselves to death, why didn't they use that time to change their hearts and minds? The answer is that they were too dead in their hearts to contemplate change. So, remember this: you either die to self, or you die in destruction. As long as you persist in your stubbornness and refuse to yield to God's will, progress will always remain elusive, forever beyond your grasp, and you probably will end destructively. This is why it is written in Proverbs 3:5-6 (KJV), *"Trust in the Lord with all thine heart; and lean not unto thine own understanding. In all thy ways acknowledge him, and he shall direct thy paths."* This is the key to true progress, trusting in God's wisdom rather than relying on our limited understanding.

The Israelites were stubborn, and Abraham carried someone on his journey outside the instructions of God because felt guilty. What happened in the end? They all could not step into the promises of God for their lives! If, after reading all these, you are not intentional about taking stock of your life, then you are probably not ready for the progress that God intends to bring into your life. This ultimately means you are not yet ready to be welcomed into the good life which is your promised land.

The Cost Of Ignoring Divine Guidance

There will be times when God will tell you, *"I require more of your time,"* but your carnal mind will rebel by insisting, *"I must use my time for this or that worldly pursuit."* In your little wisdom, you may foolishly believe yourself to be smarter than God. But, mark my words, a day of reckoning will come when you will be forced to confront the folly of your ways, and then you lament saying, *"What was I thinking?"*

Let's continue with Abraham's story. Remember I said earlier that being consumed by guilt and a misplaced sense of obligation, he felt compelled to care for his nephew, Lot. On the surface, it appeared to be the righteous course of action. However, the moment Abraham chose to take Lot with him on his divinely ordained journey, God ceased to speak to him. It was only a matter of time before the true nature of Lot would be revealed. That which God had foreseen about Lot, which Abraham had failed to perceive soon manifested itself. After being in ministry for a long period I have come to understand that, many times, people who present themselves as kind and virtuous are always harboring hidden evil within their hearts. If you are such a person, then I want you to know you have a responsibility to see that you rid yourself of that inner darkness.

Proverbs 9:8 (KJV) *says "Reprove not a scorner, lest he hate thee: rebuke a wise man, and he will love thee."* Do you know what this means? Have you seen several people who the moment they do something wrong and you correct them, they will immediately become angry? This is exactly what the bible is talking about. I have also realized that a foolish person may outwardly appreciate knowledge, but they do not truly value it in their heart of hearts. There is a vast chasm between mere appreciation of knowledge and genuine valuation of it. To appreciate knowledge is to say, *"My, how wise you are! I am impressed by the advice you have imparted; it has stirred pleasant emotions within me."* But to value knowledge is something altogether different and far more profound. To value knowledge is not only to appreciate it but to reshape the very fabric of your life to reflect this newfound wisdom.

Valuing knowledge transcends mere appreciation; it demands action and transformation.

The true colors of Lot's character were revealed when prosperity smiled upon him. There are certain people who you can never truly know until they come into financial abundance. When they *smell* prosperity, their genuine nature will be unveiled. Lot, in his prosperity, forgot that it was his association with Abraham that had given his life meaning and purpose. As soon as he tasted success, he began to conduct himself as though he no longer needed Abraham's guidance and protection. When conflicts arose between his servants and those of Abraham, Lot failed to defend his uncle's honor. Instead, he approached Abraham with false humility, saying, *"My dear uncle, let us not quarrel, for we are family. You go your way, and I shall go mine."* Abraham, in his God-given wisdom, responded, *"Lot, choose whichever portion of the land your heart desires, and I shall content myself with what remains."* In this situation, a truly grateful and righteous man would have declared,

11

"Father, I shall never forsake you! Wherever your path leads, there I shall follow." He should have honored Abraham as his father, rebuked his servants, and commanded them to be submissive to Abraham in all things since Abraham was the father figure in His life. But what did Lot do? He lifted his eyes, looked at the green plains filled with opportunity, and chose that which appeared most prosperous to his carnal mind.

Lot foolishly followed the grass that was greener in the land of Sodom and Gomorrah, failing to realize that it is not a man's physical location that defines his destiny. Rather, it is the blessings of God that determine his destiny, progress, and stepping into the promised land. Well, Abraham, in his humility, chose the seemingly barren land yet their outcomes were as different as *Day* and *Night*: the man who went for the lush and promising territory soon lost everything, while the one who chose the barren land prospered beyond measure. Why? Because it is not the place that matters, but the individual who carries the blessing within them. Abraham bore within his very being the divine blessing that could transform even the most desolate wilderness into a fruitful field!

When you read further in that scripture you will see that Lot's choices led him down a path of utter destruction. He lost everything, his sheep, camels, and all his wealth when God's judgment fell upon Sodom. Even when the Lord in His infinite mercy sent angels to warn Lot of the impending doom, it was only due to Abraham's fervent intercession that Lot was spared. The heavenly messenger said to Lot, in Genesis 19:17 (KJV) *"Flee for your life! Take nothing with you, and do not look back!"* At the end of the day, Lot who had once dwelt in luxurious palaces now found himself reduced to living in a cave, where his daughters, driven to desperation by their circumstances later committed an unspeakable sin by raping their father. Why did such tragedy befall him? Because when a person stubbornly refuses to heed God's voice, they inevitably become an object of mockery and derision.

When you compare the life of Lot and that of the Israelites, the need to reevaluate your life should dawn on you. It doesn't matter what you already have in this life or the heights you may have attained, you cannot go about boasting- if you fail to comprehend and submit to God's principles and commandments you are heading for destruction. You may indeed be a mighty soldier, but if you don't walk in God's ways, you will surely become a victim of your rebellion.

Beloved, let's learn from these examples and resolve to walk in obedience to God's divine guidance. This is the only true path of progress that will lead to the fulfillment of destiny and the attainment of THE *GOOD LIFE* He has prepared for every one of us.

CHAPTER TWO

DIVINE REVELATIONS AND YOUR PROGRESS

"God's path may seem foolish to man, but those who trust His ways will find doors of blessings where others see none."

The Wisdom Of Appearing Foolish For God

The thing about God's ways and His operations is that they often don't make sense to man. Sometimes, following God's way will make you look foolish in the eyes of everybody, but if you appear to be a fool for God, soon you will be full of God and all that He has for you. When you plan your life around your strength, you can be sure you will eventually end up in wretchedness. When you rely on your tactics and senses, you may find temporary success, but eventually, it leads to emptiness. However, if you build your life around God's blessing, even the wretched can become wealthy.

When God's word and instruction come, it will often require some form of adjustment, and when you respond to that adjustment, you will experience a shift in your spirit. Then, things will begin to shift in your favor- God could go ahead of you into your future to close doors you shouldn't access. Some people, believers even, walked through such [wrong] doors, and that led to the eventual pitiful state of their lives. You may wonder, *"Why would God allow His people to enter that wrong door?"* Well, I have discovered that in most cases, He may have given an instruction that was ignored or disobeyed. At other times, it may not have been disobedience; the enemy simply intensified the warfare against such a person, but they failed to recognize it and approach it with the intensity required.

For example, if you dream about death- yours or of a loved one- you need to pray against it seriously. It could take you about three weeks of consistent fervent prayers to see that dream averted. At this time, if someone, perhaps Satan himself, comes to offer you a million-dollar job opportunity, what would you do? Reject the job because nothing is worth more than your life, right? Of course! Only when you are sure that dream is averted can you begin to give attention to other things. You would reject the job and go to Zion. The Bible tells us upon Mount Zion there shall be deliverance, but the challenge is that deliverance requires consistency. Dreams are not evil; in truth, it means God has given you access to the spiritual realm to see what is happening- what Satan is trying to do. But know that when you have a dream, the verdict is not final until you speak. You have a say in the matter.

These are practical ways to apply the blessings of God in your life so that you don't just go about shouting, *"I'm blessed, I'm blessed!"* without seeing the evidence in your life. When you have a dream, it's a blessing to see what the enemy is trying to do. It's an opportunity for you to intercede, to pray, and to declare victory over the plans of darkness. Don't just see the dream as a threat; see it as an invitation from God to rise and reverse the enemy's plans before they manifest. God's blessings are meant to proliferate in your life, but they require application and action. So, as you respond to the revelation God gives you, whether through His word, a dream, or a prophetic message, be diligent and consistent.

The revelation for you here is that God has already positioned you for blessing, but it's now up to you to step into it fully by aligning your life with His purpose and His promises. Do you remember what Psalm 23:1-3 (KJV) says? *"The Lord is my shepherd; I shall not want. He maketh me to lie down in green pastures: he leadeth me beside the still waters. He restoreth my soul: he leadeth me in the paths of righteousness for his name's sake."* This is a reminder that when we allow God to lead us as our shepherd, He guides us to places of peace, restoration, and righteousness. It's not just about following blindly, but trusting in His wisdom and timing, even when it doesn't make sense to our human understanding. So, if you have a negative dream and you do nothing about it, it means God has shown you the future and given you a warning but you failed to act. Will you then blame God if that negative dream comes to pass? Of course not! It only came to pass because you refused to do something about it even after God's warning.

Divine Warnings And Your Destiny

Taking Your Life and Destiny Seriously

Remember Joseph interpreting the dreams of two men while he was in Prison, one of whom was destined to die? Joseph interpreted their dreams and gave the man with the bad dream three days. Now, why three days? Because the dream came too late, and those three days had a spiritual significance. When dealing with the things of the spirit, numbers like *Three* and *Seven* hold deep meanings in the spiritual realm; 3 represents divine completeness, and 7 represents spiritual perfection. When you understand spiritual numeration, you will realize that where *threes* work, *sevens* also work. That's why Jesus couldn't stay in the grave for more than *three* days, and Jonah was in the belly of the whale for *three* days. Also, when you multiply 7 by 3, you get 21 which means there are 3 *sevens* in 21 days and 7 *threes* in 21 days. Do you see why people go on a 21-day prayer and fasting? There is almost no spiritual challenge that you cannot surmount with this principle if you can take a 21-day fast seriously.

Let's go back to Joseph. After interpreting the dream, the man had three days, and in those three days, he could have reversed the outcome of his dream, but he ignored it, and on the third day, the dream was fulfilled. Sometimes, when I prophesy and tell some people that death is hunting them, they get upset and ask, "*Why are you saying that?*" God knows the mindset of people; sometimes He allows you to see the danger yourself in a dream. I want to make it clear that when God shows you something in the spirit, you must take it seriously. He also gives you time, often 21 days, to reverse the situation if it is negative.

What should you do in those 21 days? Fast and pray! This is how you come to Mount Zion to receive deliverance.

I repeat, if God shows you a dream where you see yourself naked or in danger, take time to reverse it through fasting and prayer. Otherwise, the negative outcome will manifest just as it did for the chief baker in Joseph's story. When the day came, Pharaoh called for the two men, and he was hanged, just as Joseph had interpreted. This principle applies to all areas of our lives, So don't ever ignore a dream, especially if it's negative. Otherwise, it will happen and when it does, it won't just affect you, but your family as well. For some, God may be saying, "*Serve Me, and I will exchange your service for your life.*" Remember the scripture in Exodus 23:25-26 (KJV): "*And ye shall serve the Lord your God, and he shall bless thy bread and thy water; I will take sickness away from the midst of thee. There shall nothing cast their young, nor be barren, in thy land: the number of thy days I will fulfill.*" If you choose to become wise in yourself (which is actually foolishness) and decide to ignore this instruction, then you have failed to understand that to win the fight against the spirit of death, you have to increase your commitment to God.

Many times, when the enemy makes you feel you don't have to go to church, you have to tone down on your giving to or service in the house of God, and so on, he is only trying to trap you. You may say, '*Well, I need to spend time with my family, I need to go to dinner with my family and I need to be there for them*'. Yes, spend time with your family and enjoy dinner, but don't neglect the things of God. If the enemy succeeds in taking your life, for example, who will be here with your family? Just think about that! When I teach these principles, those who are less spiritual, those who are stuck in their ways, usually don't understand. They keep thinking, "*Why should I spend so much time in the house of God, why should I give so much, why should I serve so much?* But they don't realize that it's not about just being in church and serving in church; it's actually about putting yourself in a place where the enemy's schemes against you will never be able to materialize.

Beloved of God, I truly counsel and warn you from my heart: when God shows you something in the spirit, take it seriously. Don't let pride, laziness, or ignorance stop you from securing your life and destiny. You can truly step into "*the good life*", "*the promised land*", "*the life of blessings*" and even more. The blessing is in your hands, but you must act on it by following God even when it seems foolish. If you cannot secure your destiny and glory by following God devotedly and taking divine warnings and revelations seriously, then you will always be a casualty of the enemy's tactics. Joel 2:32 (KJV), already tells "*And it shall come to pass, that whosoever shall call on the name of the Lord shall be delivered: for in mount Zion and in Jerusalem shall be deliverance, as the Lord hath said, and in the remnant whom the Lord shall call.*" So learn to call on Him, even if it will take fasting and prayer. Don't be lazy or you will never step into THE GOOD LIFE

Turning Verdicts Into Blessings

A Key To The Good Life

Isaiah 38:1-5 (KJV): "*In those days was Hezekiah sick unto death. And Isaiah the prophet, the son of Amoz, came unto him, and said unto him, Thus saith the LORD, Set thine house in order: for thou shalt die, and not live. Then Hezekiah turned his face toward the wall and prayed unto the LORD, And said, Remember now, O LORD, I beseech thee, how I have walked before thee in truth and with a perfect heart, and have done that which is good in thy sight. And Hezekiah wept sore. Then came the word of the LORD to Isaiah, saying, Go, and say to Hezekiah, Thus saith the LORD, the God of David thy father, I have heard thy prayer, I have seen thy tears: behold, I will add unto thy days fifteen years."*

In this story, when Isaiah delivered the message from God that Hezekiah was going to die, do you realize that Hezekiah didn't resist or even argue with the prophet? Instead, he turned to God in humility and reminded Him of his service and faithfulness. He didn't argue with Isaiah, but he spoke to God from his heart and said, *"Lord, remember how I have served you."* And what did God do? He reversed the verdict of death and added 15 more years to Hezekiah's life. The lesson here is that dedicated service to God has the power to change even a sentence of death. Hezekiah's story teaches that when you serve God with a sincere heart, it's possible to reverse any and every negative decree pronounced against your life. The key is service; you can serve your way into a blessing and serve your way out of an evil verdict. There is no way you will not be able to live THE GOOD LIFE if you understand and employ this principle every day of your life

Now, let's move to the message in Hebrews 3:15, where the Bible says in Hebrews 3:15 (KJV), *"While it is said, To day if ye will hear his voice, harden not your hearts, as in the provocation."* This is important because it tells us to be sensitive to God's voice.

When God speaks, especially in times like these, when death, corruption, persecution, and demonic perversions are prevalent, it's very crucial to respond with a swift and open heart because God intends to bring you out of a life of conflict, warfare, and complications. He is leading you to cross over into a life of abundance and peace. But we all have our responsibility as individuals to hear and respond to God's voice when He speaks. I cannot *obey for* you, you cannot *obey for* me; everybody must be ready to pay their price for the good life.

Today is a critical moment to make that decision for your life, whether to follow God's voice or to continue to live in stubbornness. The people of Israel heard God's voice when He delivered them from Egypt under Moses, but they didn't let His voice preserve them in the wilderness. They witnessed miracles, and they were delivered, but many of them were not preserved because of their rebellion. They didn't enter the Promised Land! Similarly, you may have experienced God's deliverance in your life, but the preservation comes through obedience, a humble heart, and following His instructions especially instructions that come through His prophet over your life.

God wants to preserve you so He's showing you signs, through losses, through dreams, through moments of reflection. Do not ignore these warnings, because this only leads to wandering in the wilderness longer than necessary, but God wants to bring you into the land flowing with milk and honey so you must stop relying on your understanding, strength, wisdom, and qualifications. Sometimes, we are too confident in our intelligence and strength, but you must never forget that it is not the labor of a man that makes Him rich or successful; it is the blessings of God.

Just in case as you are reading this and you are someone who has children, I want you to understand that securing God's blessing over your life is also securing protection for your children's destiny. If you joke with your life and God's revelations you are jeopardizing their destinies. You won't always be there for them, but if you have God's blessing, He will be there to comfort, guide, protect, and even provide for them. As you transition in this season, pray and ask God to create in you a clean heart, ask for a humble heart that is responsive to His voice. Say to Him *"Father, remove this stony heart and give me a heart of flesh, a heart that is sensitive and obedient to Your voice."*

I want you to declare today "*Father, in the name of Jesus, thank You for this day, the day You have made for my appointed transition. I reject any verdict of death and destruction over my life, and I choose to follow Your voice into the land of blessings and the good life.*" Don't just pray this prayer carelessly and mindlessly; be intentional. Let your prayer be one of humility, asking for a heart that seeks God's will above all else, knowing that His blessing is what secures your life and the future of your loved ones.

Psalm 51:10 (KJV), **"Create in me a clean heart, O God; and renew a right spirit within me."**

CHAPTER THREE

YOUR CHOICES WILL GUIDE YOU TO ABUNDANCE

"The world's blessings come with sorrow, but God's blessings bring rest and joy.

Contend For Understanding

Choosing Between Life's Burdens And The Yokes Of God

The scripture says, in Proverbs 10:22 that the blessings of God make us rich and add no sorrow to it. This means that the blessings of the Lord are not like the blessings of the world. The blessings of the world come with pressure, toiling, suffering, sorrows, and more but the blessings of the Lord come with rest, peace, and joy. This is why you must learn to choose the ways and yokes of God far more than any other things else.

"The blessings of the Lord are the signature of God upon the mind of man, enabling him to understand life, comprehend it, and interpret it

in such a way that he can apply it."

Has it ever occurred to you that you don't fail an exam just by not attending classes? Rather you fail an exam because you don't understand the subject. Yes, you could attend class for a whole year, but you will only succeed if you understand the subject. Likewise, as believers, we often don't fail simply because we aren't born again or because we don't go to church; most believers fail simply because they don't understand the principles of God's Kingdom. And those who understand them fail to apply them to their lives daily and consistently. Note this: *"Understanding isn't true understanding until it leads to application"*. When it comes to the blessings of God, you must always strive to understand it so you can apply it effectively.

The question is: *How do I apply it to my life?* Don't forget, the bible says *"The labor of the foolish man wearies him, not because there's no labor, but because he doesn't understand how to go to the city."*(Ecclesiastes 10:15) So, show me a believer whose life is unproductive, and I will show you a believer who is ignorant of the kingdom's principles and the basic rudiments of its operations.

Here is something you must understand about blessings. Jesus said, *"Come unto me, all ye that labor and are heavy laden, and I will give you rest."* (Matthew 11:28, KJV). But He didn't stop there; He also gave the key to that rest and it is found in the next verse, *"Take my yoke upon you, and learn of me; for I am meek and lowly in heart: and ye shall find rest unto your souls."* (Matthew 11:29, KJV). In other words, the yoke of Christ is the key to rest. What then is the yoke? The yoke refers to the demands of the Kingdom. In the next verse, He goes further to say *"Let me teach you, for I am gentle and humble, and you will find rest for your souls. For my yoke is easy, and my burden is light."* (Matthew 11:30, KJV)

Note that He didn't say He wouldn't give you a burden; rather He said the burden He gives is light compared to the burdens life places on you. You have a choice to either bear the burden of the Lord or carry the burden of life. Now, look at verse 29 again, *"Take my yoke upon you and learn of me."* This shows that in God's Kingdom, the key to winning is your willingness to obey His instructions– the yokes of the kingdom– as well as the humility to learn His ways every day. So, are you set for the Good life? Then get ready for obedience and learning by intentionally choosing His yoke daily. But if you choose to go with the yoke of the world, then get set for a testimony like what Job said in Job 14:1 (KJV) *"Man that is born of a woman is of few days, and full of trouble."*

Okay... To be a good learner, you must understand that there are things you have learned in life that you need to *unlearn*– old ways of doing things, old characters, old beliefs, old ideologies, and much more– so that you can begin to *relearn* what you need to find rest for your soul. You may want to say, *"Well, this is how I've always done it, this is my way."* Do you not know that the Bible says *"For my thoughts are not your thoughts, neither are your ways my ways, saith the Lord. For as the heavens are higher than the earth, so are my ways higher than your ways, and my thoughts than your thoughts."* (Isaiah 55:8-9, KJV). From this scripture, you should realize that choosing your way over God's way is completely unwise and will ultimately lead to destruction!

We see this exemplified in the lives of people like Lot who chose the green land and went there, ignoring the blessings of God which flowed from the life of Abraham towards him. At the end of the day, the man who stayed in the *dry place* ended up interceding for the one who went to the *green place*, ultimately leading to Lot losing everything while Abraham continually increased in every area of his life.

It's worth noting that when a spiritual person releases a blessing upon anybody, whether that person is saved or not, the blessing will be manifest in their lives. However, the unsaved person may acquire material things and end up in eternity without God. This is how powerful the blessings of God are. When it is upon your life, you will find yourself prospering and moving from one level to another, saved or not.

This is why you mustn't treat with levity a minister's– a true minister's– pronouncement of God's blessings upon you. Now, most people don't know this and may never say it out loud, but it is said that the founders of Dubai received a blessing from a Jewish rabbi. Can you imagine that? That's why, even though Dubai is a Muslim country, you will find some shops selling crosses. One of my favorite pendants is a cross which I bought from a shop there, something you probably won't find in the US. It's a 21-carat gold pendant with scriptures on it, and these scriptures change every time you glance at it.

The Danger Of Misplaced Sentiment And Affection

One thing that you should not miss in the life of Abraham and Lot, which we discussed earlier, is that although Lot lost everything in the end, Abraham also lost a lot because, for years, Abraham didn't enjoy the intimate fellowship he'd always had with God since Lot was with him. Why? Because he had a misplaced affection and sentiment by taking Lot along. The Lord may have given him signs, *"Abraham, leave this man alone, let this boy go,"* but Abraham refused, and God couldn't force him, just the same way God may be giving you instruction concerning your job, a friend, a relationship, your attachment to money and material things, that you need to let go, but you have refused to heed. And God cannot force you because He created us with the ability to choose.

This wasn't just Abraham; the same terrible mistake almost happened to Isaac too. He had a misplaced sentiment and affection for Esau. While God intended that Jacob would carry the blessing, Isaac wanted to give Esau the blessing over a bowl of meal, because he didn't hear or seek God. He did not need that meal anyway, but there is a vital lesson here: there are several levels of blessings and dimensions of the good life that you may never be able to enter if you do not learn the power of seeds and sacrifices. Yes, several blessings can never rest on you if it is not provoked by sacrifices.

Let's go back to Abraham. He kept the boy Lot until he almost missed his opportunity. But the Bible tells us that finally, Abraham called him and said, *'OK, you can go,'* after their herdsmen had had a series of quarrels. Now, this is the point I have been trying to get to, the amazing part of it all: as soon as Lot left Abraham, the Bible says that God spoke to Abraham, *"And the Lord said unto Abram, after that Lot was separated from him, Lift up now thine eyes, and look from the place where thou art northward, and southward, and eastward, and westward: For all the land which thou seest, to thee will I give it, and to thy seed for ever."* (Genesis 13:14-15, KJV). Child of God, you must be careful not to be led by your feelings, sentiments, affections, or any other misguided emotions. Or else, you will never be able to step into your promised land or the life that God intends for you!

Some Ways That Wrong Sentiments And Affections Hinder Destiny Include:

● **Distraction from Divine Purpose**

Worldly attachments– even to good things like family, career, or personal ambitions– can become distractions from fulfilling God's specific calling. In Luke 9:59-62, Jesus cautions us on the need for undivided focus in following Him. When you allow your legitimate concerns to take precedence over your spiritual responsibilities, they will divert your attention from pursuing God's purpose. Ultimately, these distractions will delay your spiritual growth and prevent you from stepping fully into your destiny.

● **Compromise of Values**

When affections outside God's will dominate you, they will lead

WELCOME TO THE GOOD LIFE

to compromises in your spiritual values. Think about Lot who chose the fertile plains of Sodom because of its material benefits and ignored the moral dangers of the city. His legitimate desire for prosperity led to spiritual compromise, which eventually endangered his family. When you prioritize worldly desires above God's instructions, you will end up making ethical compromises that will take you off the path of your God-given destiny.

- **Emotional Entanglement**

Sentiments such as fear, love, or attachment to people and things outside God's plan also entangle us emotionally because they can create inner conflicts, and cloud our judgment. For example, do you remember Samson's love for Delilah in Judges 16? This attachment caused him to ignore God's warnings. His affection, though legitimate, blinded him to the spiritual danger and eventually led to his downfall.

- **Delay in Spiritual Growth**

Even legitimate ambitions, like pursuing higher education, relationships, or wealth, have the power to lead you to stagnation if they overshadow the pursuit of God's will for your life. The story of the rich young ruler in Matthew 19:16-22 shows us this. He was morally upright but couldn't give up his wealth to follow Jesus. This means his attachment to material things hindered him from advancing spiritually. In the same vein, when worldly sentiments and desires become idols in your heart, they will slow down or even prevent the character formation necessary to step into God's ultimate plans for your life.

In essence, never forget that even legitimate worldly affections can hinder your destiny when they fall outside of God's for you.

Dryness To Abundance

The Bible tells us in Genesis 26 that there was a severe famine overshadowing the land, just as it had happened before in Abraham's time. "*And there was a famine in the land, besides the first famine that was in the days of Abraham. And Isaac went unto Abimelech king of the Philistines unto Gerar. And the Lord appeared unto him, and said, Go not down into Egypt; dwell in the land which I shall tell thee of Sojourn in this land, and I will be with thee, and will bless thee; for unto thee, and unto thy seed, I will give all these countries, and I will perform the oath which I sware unto Abraham thy father.*" (Genesis 26:1-3, KJV)

So, God was practically saying "*If you stay here, I will empower you.*" This is another importance of God's blessing resting upon you. *The blessing* means to empower someone to succeed in everything they do. In essence, God was saying to Isaac, '*I will bless you, I will empower you.*' And what would happen? This *empowerment* would give him the land. He didn't say it would give him houses and other material things; rather, He said the *power* would give him the land. Contextually, the land is symbolic of industries, fields, and areas of life; God intends that you will own all these. The truth is, there are certain industries that God is preparing you to own, but if you give in to the famine and run away from the place that God has asked you to stay, then you may never be able to step into that dimension of blessing.

Isaac was about to make a wrong move by going to Egypt because he believed that there would be supply there. Have you not seen people who ran away from their own countries because they felt the economy was bad, only for them to get overseas and begin to suffer in an even worse way? You have to know that all you need is to be where God wants you to be! God said to Isaac, "*Stay and I will bless you,*" Don't forget God had already promised Abraham, "*And I will make thy seed to multiply as the stars of heaven, and will give unto thy seed all these countries; and in thy seed shall all the nations of the earth be blessed; Because that Abraham obeyed my voice, and kept my charge, my commandments, my statutes, and my laws.*" (Genesis 26:4-5, KJV) But for Isaac to enjoy that blessing, he had to make sure he obeyed the Lord because it was only through obedience that dry land could turn into a place of abundance. I may not be fully aware of what you are going through but I sense in my Spirit that right now, the Lord is saying to tell you once again, *"I will bless you, and I will cause you to dominate many areas of life."*

As you walk in obedience to God's word and align yourself with His principles, know that you are positioning yourself to receive His blessings. But, more than that, you become a channel through which His blessing can flow to others. When your choices are guided by God's wisdom, they will not only lead you to abundance but will also create opportunities for others to experience God's goodness through your life.

In essence, your choices will indeed guide you to abundance, only if those choices are in line with God's will and ways for your life. So, choose to bear the light burden of Christ rather than the heavy burdens of the world, and choose to let go of misplaced sentiments and affections that may be holding you back from God's best for you.

If you can walk in obedience, your life may look like dry land right now, but in just a matter of time, those seemingly dry places will be turned into a fruitful field flowing with milk and honey in the mighty name of Jesus.

I need you to take some time and meditate on Deuteronomy 8:18 because you are about to step into the GOOD LIFE *"But thou shalt remember the Lord thy God: for it is he that giveth thee power to get wealth, that he may establish his covenant which he sware unto thy fathers, as it is this day."* (Deuteronomy 8:18, KJV).

CHAPTER FOUR

MOVING FROM OBSCURITY TO PROMINENCE

"Let God shape your mindset, and you'll walk in abundance beyond the natural realm."

Walking In With The Divine Mentality

hen you read the stories of men like Louis Vuitton who went from being a stranded traveler to a global celebrity, you should be encouraged because I know that your life may not be all that you desire right now, and things may not be as beautiful as you want. However, I want you to know God is saying to you today, "I'm training you to take over." This means God is preparing you for something grand, something beyond your wildest dreams, and He is molding, shaping, and equipping you for a destiny that will shake the very foundations of this world. Do you know why? Because right from the foundations of the world He desires that you will enjoy THE GOOD LIFE. Jeremiah 29:11 says, "For I know the thoughts that I think toward you, saith the Lord, thoughts of peace, and not of evil, to give you an expected end."

The journey from obscurity to prominence isn't smooth; it is filled with trials, tribulations, and moments where you will feel like giving up. But those struggles are your training ground because God doesn't just want to give you success; He wants to prepare you to handle that success with wisdom, integrity, and humility. Today, by the power of God, I authorize you to cross over to the place of rest in the mighty name of Jesus. I declare that it's time to enter your Promised Land and step into the abundance that God has prepared for you, in the name of Jesus. The Scripture says in Hebrews 4:9-10 (KJV), *"There remaineth therefore a rest to the people of God. For he that is entered into his rest, he also hath ceased from his own works, as God did from his."* It's time to cease your striving and enter into God's divine rest, where His power works mightily through you and empowers you to live the GOOD LIFE.

In the previous chapter, we talked about Isaac. Now, let me ask you a question: when Isaac stayed in that land during the time of famine, what did he do? Did he look for a job? Did he suddenly start begging? NO! He stayed in that land. He held onto the promise of God which He had pronounced, *"I'll bless you,"* and indeed he was blessed.

One of the things that the blessing of the Lord will do is that it will give you a mindset that is far beyond the mind of a natural man. If you keep thinking like the average man, you will never be able to see things the way God sees them, and you will not be able to work with Him and see His blessings transformed into material prosperity, peace, love, joy, happiness, and other wondrous things in your life. So, we can say that *"God gave him a divine mentality connected to divinity and that led to his dignity and glorification among men"*. This mentality we are talking about is a supernatural perspective that sees beyond the natural realm and taps into the limitless resources of heaven.

This land was so dry that people couldn't farm because there was no rain. But because the blessing of the Lord gave Isaac a different mentality, he was able to function far above the limitations of that land. Now, there were three things having this divine mentality by the blessings of God did for him. Let us break it down and see how it can transform your life, just like it did for Isaac.

Number 1

Seeing Through God's Eyes

A divine mentality is a mentality that sees with the eyes and mind of God. It is the mentality that perceives what others cannot see, and when men look at you and say, "*There's a casting down,*" your mindset will be able to say, "*I Don't see casting down, what I see is a lifting up!*" Why? Because you are viewing life through God's lens. This is a supernatural vision that penetrates through the fog of circumstances and sees the glorious future God has prepared for you. Through this level of transformation in your mind, God allows you to see what your generation cannot see, He enables you to think differently from the world and He allows you to see possibilities amid impossibilities.

Think about it: during the famine, God said to him "*Stay.*" And when Isaac stayed, he began to see through the eyes and mind of God– what was the mind of God in this situation? God said to him, "*Everyone is running away because this place is dry, but you don't have to run away because there is blessing and glory for you here*" You may want to say to me "*Sir, but I cannot see the blessing.*" I want you to look inside you, the blessing is inside you!

In simple terms, God was saying to Isaac "*If you stay here, I'm going to cause what's in you to affect the land, and what will happen is that the land will respond to you, and because of you the land will be blessed to produce.*" Can you understand the magnitude of this promise? God was literally saying that the blessing within him had the power to transform not just his life, but his environment.

So, it doesn't matter if you are in a barren land; the moment you step into that land, the land is supposed to respond to the blessings of God upon your life, and suddenly begin to produce abundance. Read Genesis 26:3-4 again in the KJV, *"Sojourn in this land, and I will be with thee, and will bless thee; for unto thee, and unto thy seed, I will give all these countries, and I will perform the oath which I sware unto Abraham thy father; And I will make thy seed to multiply as the stars of heaven, and will give unto thy seed all these countries; and in thy seed shall all the nations of the earth be blessed."*

I pray that the next 20 moves you make between now and the end of this year will be directly connected to the eyes and mind of God in the mighty name of Jesus.

You may want to purchase some properties, but God will close the door. Don't complain. Instead, learn to view the situation through God's eyes, and you will realize that there's probably a death, a debt, or any kind of trouble in that house. And God wouldn't want you to deal with that, or be affected by it. No matter how good it looks, He may have something better in mind. So, He will say to you, *"Wait until I flush out the debt and death in this property or until I bring the right person to you so you can acquire it without all the sweat and complications."*

This divine mentality will teach you to see that most of the time, God's *'Nos'* are a blessing in disguise. When God closes certain doors it's actually because you are too blessed to become a victim of a satanic open door or a contaminated place. So, don't you dare compromise your divine destiny for temporary gratification. Remember Proverbs 14:12 (KJV) warns us that *"There is a way which seemeth right unto a man, but the end thereof are the ways of death."* You must learn to trust in God's wisdom, even when it doesn't make sense to your natural mind.

I pray for a sensitive spiritual life for you, that within your dreams, God will show up and speak to you in the name of Jesus. May your spiritual senses be sharpened, and your discernment heightened, so that you can perceive the subtle nudgings of the Holy Spirit and be able to take advantage of the divine mentality he is providing for you today in the mighty name of Jesus!

Number 2

The Breath Of God Coupled With Empowering Faith And Stability

Now, let's talk about the second aspect of this divine mentality. A Divine mentality is the mentality that enjoys the breath of God. It provides you with the faith and stability needed to benefit from that which God has in store for you. When I talk about the breath of God, I mean the very life force of the Almighty, infusing you with supernatural power and faith in your mind.

In Hebrew, it is the *"ruach"* of God breathing upon you and giving you the faith and stability necessary to benefit from the field, the land. God said, *"Stay."* But if you don't have the faith to stay, you'll be scared away by the famine. Let me break it down for you: Perhaps God has told you, *"Buy the house,"* but the naysayers are saying, *"You don't have good credit."* Well, it is good to have good credit, but I promise you, when this divine mentality is at work in you, your eyes will see beyond your bank account or credit store, to realize that God has good credit. So, whenever He says a thing, He will definitely bring it to pass. Don't limit yourself to the systems of this world; when God's breath is upon you, you are meant to operate in a different realm completely. The Scripture declares in 2 Corinthians 5:7 (KJV), *"For we walk by faith, not by sight."* Your faith, empowered by God's breath, has the power to move mountains and open doors that no man can shut.

In Mark 11:22 Jesus said, *"Have faith in God,"* but when you go to the Greek, it says more than that; it says, *"Have the God-kind of faith."* This is the kind of faith that moves mountains, parts seas, and raises the dead. It's a faith that defies logic and laughs in the face of impossibility. *How can I have the God kind of faith?* You may ask. It is when the *"ruach Elohim"* breathes upon your mind. Even when everything around you says, *"This thing can't work,"* the breath of God in you will tell you, *"Though your beginning be small, your latter end shall greatly increase."* Job 8:7. Child of God, don't you dare despise the day of small beginnings, for God is about to do something miraculous in your life.

Number 3

The Touch Of God That Turns Adversity Into Prosperity

The third aspect is that the divine mentality is the mind that receives the touch of God which empowers one to turn adversity and austerity into lifelong prosperity. I am talking about the transformative power of the Almighty, turning your trials into triumphs and your struggles into stepping stones to greatness so that you can get into the good life that God intends for you to live, beyond all doubt.

When your mind receives the touch of God, it gives you the ability to look at things that seem adverse, unfavorable, and fruitless, and transform them because on the flip side of adversity is advertisement. With the touch of God on your mind, you will always be able to create opportunities and glory where other people experience obstacles, failures, and dead ends. This is because the touch of God Has empowered you to turn your trials into testimonies that will glorify His name.

Here's an example: when Moses and the Israelites were traveling, they encountered a place where the water was deadly. Every traveler who drank from that water became sick and eventually died. So, people abandoned the water and nobody wanted it.

Years later, when the children of Israelites crossed the Red Sea, they came around that place where the water was bitter. By this time, they were very thirsty and they cried out to the Lord, "*Oh God, what is going to happen to us? We are thirsty.*" And God told Moses, "*Take that wood and throw it into the water.*" Can you see that no scientist is more scientifically advanced than God? What's the correlation between wood and water? Absolutely nothing! But when the blessings of God are at work, logic is irrelevant!

So, Moses threw the wood into the water, and it became drinkable. I declare that what causes sickness and death for others will bring nourishment and life to you; it will bring you into a place of wealth, riches, and glory, in the name of Jesus. I see you enjoying new levels of prosperity!

It only takes one move! Others may have tried a thousand times and failed, but for you, it will only take one move! One move and you will start the business, purchase the property, succeed, and step into the good life, in the mighty name of Jesus!

I declare that you will take the same things others abandoned and turn them into sources of blessing, in the name of Jesus!

Rely On God And Not On False Security

Genesis 26:11-12 "*And Abimelech charged all his people, saying, He that toucheth this man or his wife shall surely be put to death. Then Isaac sowed in that land, and received in the same year an hundredfold: and the Lord blessed him.*

From this scripture, we can see that Abimelech made a public proclamation, telling everyone not to touch Isaac or his wife. At this point, he had recognized the blessing that was on Isaac. When God touches your mind, you will begin to gain recognition. But a caution you should take is that you must never allow the enemy to hinder your close fellowship with God by any means, or you'll lose your protection. It doesn't matter how wealthy you are, if you aren't protected, you are vulnerable to the gimmicks of Satan.

Now before verse 11, let me explain to you why Abimelech made the decree.

In Genesis 26:6-9, just like Abraham did before him, Isaac just came into the land of Abimelech and he was scared for his life because of his beautiful wife, Rebekah. He didn't want them to kill him to claim his wife. So, he told the men of Gerar that Rebekah was his sister instead. But King Abimelech later saw Isaac showing affection toward Rebekah and realized she was his wife. In Genesis 26:9-10 Abimelech confronted Isaac for lying, pointing out that someone could have taken Rebekah, thereby bringing guilt and curses upon the land. So, Isaac explained his fear of being killed because of her and admitted to Abimelech that this was the reason for his lying.

What you need to understand here is that God put the fear of Isaac in the heart of Abimelech, the same fear that Jacob talked about in Genesis 31:42 (KJV) when he said *"Except the God of my father, the God of Abraham, and the fear of Isaac,..."* But Abimelech didn't realize that Isaac was a man whose mind had been touched by God, and so they were not equals. Know that so long as you stay with God, your equality with all those looking down on you will soon become inequality. They may have thought you were on the same level, but you are about to rise. In this life, many people may be fine with you so long as they think you are equals. But the moment your story changes for good, you will be shocked at how the hypocrisy of men is revealed.

That's why you need to be properly protected. But you must never count on the promises of protection from ungodly people. Never count on the security your job promises you. You might worship that job and even commit your life to it, but one day, they will drop you like a hot potato and you will be shocked. In this life, you may do everything right, but just don't rise too high if you don't want terrible and wicked enemies.

Did you get that? You can do everything right, just don't rise too high except you are ready for the warfare that comes with it. The moment you start rising in the company, the same people who praised you may turn against you. There was a lady I ministered to who worked in a bank where the president was the obstacle to her promotion because he wanted someone else in a rich guy's circle to get the job. But when the blessing of the Almighty is upon you, no man can stop your rising; they may fight you, but as long as the protection of God is upon you, they will never be able to prevail against you. Psalm 75:6-7 (KJV) tells us *"For promotion cometh neither from the east, nor from the west, nor from the south. But God is the judge: he putteth down one, and setteth up another."* Your promotion doesn't come from man; it comes from God Almighty!

If you count on false security, eventually you will not just be downgraded, but you will be defrauded and defeated. As soon as your life starts reflecting the touch of God, you will be shocked at who is willing to sell you out for the price of a slave. So, I declare over you today, no weapon formed against you shall prosper and every tongue that rises against you in judgment, you shall condemn. This is your heritage as a servant of the Lord. Your vindication comes from Him. You are more than a conqueror through Christ who loves you. You are the head and not the tail, above only and not beneath.

Remember, child of God, you are not walking this path alone; the God who called you is faithful to complete the good work He has begun in you. So, instead of trusting in men for your security, it is better to trust in the Lord who is your shepherd (Psalm 23).

Hold On Tight To The Lord

When the Almighty God, in His infinite wisdom and boundless mercy, decides to elevate you to greater heights, it is of utmost importance that you, as a child of the Most High, make a conscious and unending decision to cling tightly to Him. Yes, when the

41

Lord God Almighty chooses to exalt you, you must, with all your strength and resolve, hold onto Him even more firmly than before. I want you to think about the natural reaction of a young child when tossed playfully into the air. You will see that their instinctive response is to hold on to the one carrying them tightly. Do you know why? They are scared of falling! There is nobody who goes up without the fear of coming down, and if the one who promises to hold you when you are coming down is weaker than you, then you are in trouble.

I said this to let you know that when God comes to you saying, "*I'm taking you up,*" you better respond by saying, "*Lord, if You are lifting me, then I am holding onto you like never before, and wherever You are headed, that's where I'm going too.*" Do you remember that story about Jacob wrestling with the angel? They wrestled all night long, and when Jacob finally realized who he was dealing with, he quickly held the angel and said, "*I'm not letting go unless you bless me.*" That's the kind of attitude you need to cultivate when God says He's taking you up.

Look at Psalm 27:8 (KJV): "*When thou saidst, Seek ye my face; my heart said unto thee, Thy face, Lord, will I seek.*" This verse shows us the right response to God's call. When He invites you into deeper fellowship and promises elevation, your heart's immediate reaction should be, "*Lord, I will seek Your face.*" It is foolish to boast of promotion from God and then neglect your connection with Him because no one can sustain the heights of success without maintaining a strong relationship with the One who lifts them.

You must also note that God's laws and principles of protection are very precise and powerful. He declared in Psalm 91:1 (KJV), "*He that dwelleth in the secret place of the most High shall abide under the shadow of the Almighty.*" So, if you seek protection, you must learn to dwell in God's secret place, continually seeking His presence and not moving away from Him. Part of this protection also comes through the power of your words, as verse 2 says, "*I will say of the Lord, He is my refuge and my fortress: my God; in him will I trust."* As a child of God, the words you speak over your life, declaring God as your refuge and fortress are very pivotal to your protection. Also, your tongue must declare that your spirit believes that God is your protection.

Coupled with all these, you must learn to keep the devourer away from your blessings and the major way of doing this is to honor God with your tithe. When you read Malachi 3:10, the word of God tells us that when you bring the tithe into the storehouse, God will rebuke the devourer for your sake. How about when you withhold the tithe? Then you are inviting the devourer to take what belongs to you. Beloved, if you think you are too sophisticated to follow God's financial principles of paying your tithe, then prepare to deal with the devourer yourself. But know this: every human being pays some form of tithe– it's a universal law. Even billionaires, who may not recognize God, understand the principle of giving back so you will sometimes see them invest in the community or donate funds to charity. As believers, God expects us to bring our tithe to His storehouse so it can be used for purposes that are beneficial to the human spirit and advancement of His kingdom.

Don't ever forget this: the devourer is always waiting, lurking and seeking an opportunity to consume your blessings and resources. If you refuse to pay your tithe, you will definitely end up paying it in several other unpleasant and even terrible ways, probably through dealing with health issues, financial loss, bad debts, etc. That's why God gives us this principle, to ensure that we live under His divine protection and providence.

Another very critical aspect of holding onto the Lord is guarding your heart against bitterness. As you rise higher in life, the air becomes *thinner*, just like it does in the physical world. So, if you keep going up and your heart is filled with bitterness, that bitterness can choke you when you get to a higher altitude. A little more explanation: *The higher you go, the more people will envy and oppose you. So, if you allow bitterness to take root in your heart, that bitterness will begin to affect your actions, your character, your relationship with God, and several aspects of your spiritual life.* In other words, the bitterness that you allowed to take root in your heart starts to slowly suffocate you in a very terrible way. Why not read Ephesians 4:31 (KJV) *"Let all bitterness, and wrath, and anger, and clamor, and evil speaking, be put away from you, with all malice."* Holding onto bitterness while trying to ascend in God's plan is like trying to breathe through a straw; it's impractical and ineffective.

CHAPTER FIVE

THE MYSTERY OF SOUNDS AND VICTORY IN LIFE

"Sometimes the key to unlocking your greatest victory is as simple as obeying a sound, a shout, a whisper from the Lord."

When God Takes You To The Other Side, Everything Is Different

When God prepares to take you to the other side, everything about your life begins to shift. This is because there is a great difference between where you are and where He is taking you, and understanding this difference is key to unlocking the good life of comfort, progress, and fulfillment in destiny. It's not just about moving physically or experiencing external changes; it's a deep, spiritual transformation. This transition is often marked by a sound. I will explain.

In 1 Kings 18:41, we have Elijah speaking to King Ahab, and he said, *"I hear the sound of abundance of rain."* What you need to ask yourself is *"Where did he hear this sound?"* Because, by this time, the rain had not started falling. He had not even gone to the mountain to pray for the rain to fall. In other words, this was not just a physical sound, but a prophetic indication that something in the spirit realm had shifted. The sound of rain here symbolizes the end of drought, and the cessation of pain, shame, and affliction. Before you can step into the good life, the old life of struggle, suffering, and limitation must end. And for this to happen there must be a sound in the spirit, a sound that signals the presence of God moving on your behalf.

Know that God is always at work, and as you walk with Him, you will begin to hear and be able to create the sound that announces your breakthrough. 2 Kings 13:19 explains this powerful principle better. This was not just a physical action; it was a spiritual law. In the realm of the spirit, sounds are a key component to shifting atmospheres, breaking chains, and opening doors. If you do not hear a sound, then it becomes necessary for you to create one. In the case of King Joash, Elisha was angry because he did not create enough of a sound. If he was spiritually sensitive enough, he would have known that striking the ground only three times was not sufficient to guarantee victory; more action, more sound was needed, but due to a lack of Spiritual insight, he failed! How sensitive are you? When God begins to prompt you to worship, sometimes to just shout hallelujah, or a shout of rejoicing, do you do it? Or do you begin to feel it's childish? These are the ways we most times lose the victories and breakthroughs that God intends to bring into our lives.

The spirit realm is alive with activity, and the language of that realm is sound. It's no coincidence that in moments of divine instruction, or when the heavens are about to move on behalf of God's people, there is often a sound. Read Joshua 6:3-16, and you will see that God gave Joshua instructions to march around the walls of Jericho for six days, and on the seventh day, they were to march around seven times and then raise a sound, "*a mighty shout*". This sound was even coupled with the blowing of trumpets, sounds of cymbals, and other musical instruments. Think about this for a moment, does it make any sense in the natural world? Using shouts as a war strategy? But divine instructions are not always meant to appeal to human logic. The walls of Jericho were so thick that houses were built on them, and yet a simple sound brought those formidable walls crashing down. This is exactly how it may not make sense, but I assure you that the right sound has the power to break yokes, break financial challenges, and shoot you into the good life that Christ intends for you!

This teaches us a profound lesson about obedience to divine instruction. Sometimes the solution to the most complex problems in our lives is simple, but we often miss it because it appears ridiculous. Imagine someone telling you that the secret to your breakthrough is to shout or blow a trumpet. It sounds foolish. But in the hands of God, such simple prophetic acts are very powerful tools for deliverance and breakthrough. Most people miss God's benefits because they dismiss His instructions as nonsensical. Yet, if you can obey, you will experience breakthroughs that defy human understanding. Never forget that the act of raising a sound, whether it be through prayer, praise, or prophetic declaration, is what activates the power of God in your situation because it has the power to activate and mobilize angels on your behalf. If you are sensitive in the spirit, you will know when a sound is being raised around you, and you will know how to respond to it too. So, check your life right now and examine it through the lens of the spirit; if no sound is coming then you must be proactive and raise one.

The Holy Ghost Arrived With A Sound

Acts 2:2 (KJV) "*And suddenly there came a sound from heaven as of a rushing mighty wind, and it filled all the house where they were sitting.*" This incident happened on the arrival of the Holy Spirit, when He descended on the disciples at Pentecost, there was a sound from heaven like a *"rushing mighty wind"*. And this sound signified the arrival of a new season, a season of empowerment, where the destinies of men that had been locked up were suddenly opened. Do you now see why you must be sensitive to hear the sounds of God in your life? I repeat: until you hear or raise the right sound, some things may never become yours.

The Children Of Israel Released Sounds

The story in Exodus 15:1-3 also shows us how the Israelites raised sounds that sustained their future. After crossing the Red Sea, Moses and the children of Israel sang a song of victory, declaring the greatness of God who had triumphed gloriously. Their songs were sounds that solidified their victory by reinforcing their faith in God and ensuring that their future was secured. So, when you begin to experience victories, no matter how small you must learn to solidify those victories with the right sounds. God expects you to respond to victories and breakthroughs with a sound of thanksgiving, testimonies, joy, and even laughter. Don't just keep quiet as though God has not done anything because what you may call a small win today may need your sound to become a mighty victory tomorrow.

Since the fall of man in Genesis 3:8, humanity's default sound has been negative– the sounds of sorrow, pain, and loss– which echoes throughout history, and many people live their lives in response to these negative sounds daily. This is why so many feel tired, sick, weak, and even broke. But when you step into the good life, the sound changes, just the same way that a new sound was announced when Jesus was resurrected– *a sound of triumph over death*– and this sound signified the beginning of a new life for all who believe in Him.

Beloved, as you desire to step into your destiny, you must be attuned to the sounds in the spirit realm. The sons of Issachar, as described in 1 Chronicles 12:32, *understood the times and knew what Israel should do*. You, too, must know what is happening in the spirit realm, so when there is a sound, you respond to it, and if there is no sound you raise one. This is how you will access the fullness of the good life and ensure that the blessings God has for you are not only received but also sustained.

Sound Creates Energy Or Sucks Out Energy

Another thing about sounds is that they can either energize you or drain you. In many cases, the reason people do not reach the heights God has for them is that they are not sensitive to the sounds that influence their lives positively. Instead, they are fully sensitive to the sounds that keep draining and affecting them negatively. When God calls you to the other side, to a place of breakthrough and fulfillment, there will be obstacles in your path. They may come in the form of physical barriers or even spiritual barriers. However, one thing you must not do is allow the sounds of people's complaints, criticism, fear, doubt, anxiety or even worry to fill your heart. All these are negative sounds that empower the work of darkness over your life. And as long as you keep allowing those sounds into your heart, you can forget about attaining victory or even sustaining any form of victory you may have had in the past.

In Exodus 12:38 and Exodus 32:1-5, we see the impact of the wrong sounds. The mixed multitude that left Egypt with the Israelites did not share the same dedication to God, and their voices influenced the Israelites to build the golden calf, leading them away from God's purpose. This truly illustrates that the wrong sounds, especially from those who are not in line with your destiny, will drain your energy and pull you off course in the wrong direction, ultimately leading to your destruction. This happens because the people you surround yourself with and the voices you listen to have a significant impact on your journey toward destiny whether you like it or not.

Whether you realize it or not, everything around you is speaking; even those who are silent communicate something through their actions and attitudes. The person sitting next to you and acting tired is sending a message. If you continue to look at them and focus on their weariness, their energy will begin to influence you and suddenly you also will begin to feel tired. When you look at someone who is energized and focused on God, their energy will not only influence you but will also speak to your spirit and encourage you to keep going.

In John 5:7-9, the Bible tells us about the man at the pool of Bethesda. He had been lying in that condition for 38 years. If he had continued to focus on his weakness and the fact that he had no one to help him into the pool, he would have remained in that state. But when Jesus spoke to him and told him to rise, take up his bed, and walk, the man responded to the sound of Jesus' voice, and so he was healed. What has the Lord spoken to you today? What did He tell you yesterday? When his prophet spoke to you, what did they say? Did you respond in faith? Did you allow that sound to resonate in your heart? Or did you just ignore that sound as though it was irrelevant? These are the little things we do that either accelerate or slow us down on the path of victory. So, I challenge you to take stock of all these today and learn to value these sounds more accurately.

Why do you think the Bible in Joel 3:10 instructs the weak to declare, "*I am strong*"? Why do you think the word of God says the poor should say, "*I am rich*"? It's all because the right sounds have the power to alter your life when you speak them in faith and declare them with boldness. Hence if you keep calling yourself weak, defeated, poor, broken, and useless, that's eventually who you will become because the sounds you are releasing will cause a vibration in the spiritual and invite the demonic spirits that can keep you trapped in those dejected states for life.

Don't Allow Wrong Narratives

Many people receive revelations about their destiny but fail to become what God said they would be because they do not understand the power of sounds. They allow the enemy to create a narrative around their lives, feeding them the sounds of fear, doubt, and discouragement. But Jesus constantly countered fear with faith. When the disciples panicked during the storm, Jesus' words to them were, *"Fear not"* (Matthew 14:30). It wasn't that the storm wasn't real; it was that the sound of fear had to be drowned out by the sound of faith.

To sustain the energy needed to move forward, you must be careful about the sounds you allow into your life. The wrong sounds will drain your energy and keep you stuck, but the right sounds will energize you and propel you into the good life. Surround yourself with the Word of God, worship, and the encouragement of those who are aligned with your purpose. When you focus on the right sounds, you will generate the strength to not only cross over but also thrive on the other side, living in the fullness of the good life that God has prepared for you.

CHAPTER SIX

SOUND YOUR WAY INTO VICTORY NOW!

"To hear God's voice, you must first let Him hear yours in the quiet moments of your surrender"

The Power Of Your Sound

The new phase you are seeking in your life is waiting on something specific and that is your sound. Many believers live in a realm where they misunderstand the power of their sound and personal voice. They don't understand the power that God has placed in them and this is quite a shame. Now, although outbursts, trumpet sounds, and loud shouts are very significant in the world of sound, there is a very vital and profound dimension of your sound that comes from something deeper within you. I am talking about the sound that is birthed in your quiet spirit and personal walk with God. This isn't the noise made during a time of celebration or praise; it is the frequency of your soul as you journey through life remaining faithful and focused on God every day.

The sounds that I am talking about here are the whispers of God in your spirit when you master the art of solitude and quietness

WELCOME TO THE GOOD LIFE

so that your heart can be attuned to him. Sometimes, he may lead you to pray, make a declaration, declare a prophecy over your life, or sing a song, and so on. Have you ever woken up from sleep in the morning and then there was a song in your heart throughout the whole day; and the more you sang that song the more that song blessed you? Sometimes, you will realize that if you sing any other song, your spirit will reject it and tell you to go back to that previous song. That's a personal sound. Through that song, the Lord is working in you, for you, through you, and doing so much that may not be visible to the physical eyes. All these are tools of victory through sound and you must master them.

You see, your quiet walk with God can sometimes be a weary one, and there are moments in life when the battle will seem unending and the burdens overwhelming. This is when your real sound, which is an offspring of your enduring faith, must rise. After a service one day, while having a destiny talk with my son, God instructed me to tell him, "*After you leave this office, don't let anyone hear your voice. Go lie on the altar and let God first hear your voice, if He hears your voice, then you will hear His voice.*" This powerful instruction is a very deep revelation regarding the importance of sound and you must not miss it. Many times, we tend to talk too much because we are human. Have you ever been in a period of intense fasting and prayer, and you can literally feel God's presence? What happens if you immediately start talking, laughing, and joking? You will suddenly begin to feel as though His presence and power are dissipating and leaving you to become a natural human being again.

Just take a look at those of us who are *foolish enough* to respect the spirit world. We are often the strongest, and it's not because of our physical might or intelligence, but because we understand that true power comes from our connection with God, and every sound that comes from that personal walk. Child of God, when you can grasp this spiritual principle and know how to release personal sounds that originate from your deep walk with God, then you will gain a level of strength that the natural world cannot explain. During that period, when I gave Joshua, my son, the word of the Lord, for about six days, I kept asking him to tell me what God was telling him. Do you know why? Because I knew that the personal sounds that the Lord would reveal to his heart were very key and pivotal to his destiny.

You must never play with the act of listening to God's voice and then articulating what you have heard; it is very essential. It is not enough to be aware of God's presence; you must be in constant communication with Him, and that communication is what will produce the sounds of power within your spirit.

On this side of life, you must silence pain, fear, shame, retrogression, stagnation, and non-achievement. These negative sounds are constantly trying to speak into your life, but you have the authority to silence them with your sound, and it's only you who can do that. If you don't, and you attempt to cross over to the next phase of your destiny without dealing with these issues, you will simply carry them with you, thereby prolonging the length of your calamity.

Obedience And Timing, The Keys To Ensure You Step Into The Good Life

Take a look at the book of Deuteronomy 3:23-25 where Moses begged God to let him cross over. Moses was the man of God who had performed miracles, touching dust and turning it into lice, and touching water and turning it into blood. How could a man who had seen God's power so intimately now beg to cross over? Well, the challenge is that he disobeyed God. Out of anger, he struck the rock that was supposed to bring water when God clearly instructed him to only speak to the rock. This should teach you a serious lesson concerning obedience: when God said to *speak*, God was expecting him to use "*words*," that is, sound. But he disobeyed and this cost him the promised land; he was barred from stepping into the next level.

I once went to preach somewhere, and God gave me a strange instruction. He said, *"There are many barren women and business people here stuck on the other side. I want you to put your mantle on the ground, pour oil on the ground, and call them to cross it."* Naturally, this instruction didn't make sense to me, but I obeyed. After making the announcement and following through with the mantle and oil, the results were astonishing. 41 women were trying to conceive and over 60 business people were stuck in financial hardship. The very next day, one businessman who had been waiting for a breakthrough received a call. He made a profit of 380 million Naira after six years of frustration. Over the next six months, 26 of the women became pregnant, including one woman without a womb. Imagine if I had not obeyed, or if those people had refused to believe the instruction, they obviously would have missed God's ordained time for their healing and deliverance, and maybe some of them would never have had another chance.

Strive To Carry The Ark

In Joshua 3:12-15, we have the Israelites carrying the Ark of the Covenant as they prepare to cross the Jordan River. The Ark represented the presence of God, and naturally, one might assume that the simplest way to cross the river would be to place the Ark in the water, expecting the waters to part. However, God's instructions were different. He told the priests to step into the water first, carrying the Ark on their shoulders before the waters would part. This is another story that shows the necessity of strict obedience if you want to see victory! One thing you must note is that following God's instructions is critical, but following them at the right time is even more important.

As an Apostle of God, I want you to know that carrying God's ark, which is His presence and anointing is not cheap! Truly, the weight of walking in God's anointing and serving Him is not light. There is a price to pay, and that price includes obedience, patience, extended prayer, study, and faithfulness. But when you have successfully paid this price, every sound you make, especially in prayers or declarations, will have the power to divide any river, part seas, make the moon stand still, cure diseases, and drive out demons. But you must also learn to move and do all these things according to God's timing. There will be times when God may not lead you to do any of these, and in those seasons you are to sit quietly and do nothing; you cannot move in your strength because you want to show off the miraculous power of gifts and prophecy. If you cannot wait for God's timing, then you may not witness His power and gifts flow through you. Don't think that, just because you have the anointing, you can move whenever you please– there is a divine order to everything and God's timing is a critical part of that order.

The sound of God's presence in your life gives you wisdom that brings strength. Strength is a gift from God, but it is only given to those who are in tune with His divine sound. God often gives us ridiculous instructions at ridiculous times, and we are tempted to question His logic. Why didn't God tell the Israelites to wait until the Jordan wasn't overflowing? Why did He choose the most difficult time of year, during harvest season when the river was at its highest and most dangerous? This is because God likes to show off His power in impossible situations. He is the master over bad things– evil cannot intimidate Him, and He often chooses to perform miracles in the most unlikely circumstances to demonstrate His greatness. You can be sure that no matter the opposition the enemy may bring your way, so long as you stay with God, nothing will ever be able to stop you from entering into the good and victorious life, the life of joy and all that He has ordained for you.

When God gives you an instruction, even if it seems ridiculous, trust that it is part of His miraculous plan. A wise person recognizes that God's timing is always perfect, even when it doesn't make sense in the natural world. If you miss His timing, you will miss the miracle. But if you align yourself with His timing, you will see your mountains move away, impossible situations turn around and you will eventually step into a life of victory, abundance, glory, splendor, and more.

Child of God, do you want a better life? Then it is time to master obedience and follow God's timing!

What I Carry, You Need!

It is a grave mistake to underestimate the importance of what God has placed inside of you because all of us as believers carry something unique that is needed by others. But far too many people fail to recognize the value of what they carry. They downplay their gifts, their anointing, and their purpose, thinking that what they have to offer is insignificant. But what I carry, you need; what you carry, others need. It is not pride or arrogance; it is understanding the divine assignment upon your life. This understanding is very important because it is through your assignment and all that God placed inside of you that you can step into greatness and a fulfilled life.

One of the greatest mistakes you can make is to ignore the call of God and the gifts He has placed within us. When you do that, you not only rob yourself of the fulfillment of your destiny, but you also rob others of the blessings they could receive through you. God has strategically placed people in our lives who need what we carry, so it is up to us to be faithful stewards of the gifts and anointing He has given us, recognizing that we have a responsibility to share those gifts with the world. You cannot live this way and not enjoy a life of provision, protection, and abundance. No, it doesn't work that way. The Bible says in Hebrews 6:10. *"For God is not unrighteous to forget your work and labor of love, which ye have shewed toward his name, in that ye have ministered to the saints, and do minister."*

This is the mentality we must adopt if we want to experience the fullness of the good life that God has for us. We must be willing to step out in faith, even when the timing seems wrong or the obstacles seem insurmountable. Trust that what you carry is powerful and that others need it. Be bold in releasing your gifts, and watch how God uses you to bring others into their season of victory while He continually walks you into your own.

CHAPTER SEVEN

THE POWER OF THE "I AM SET" MINDSET

"A mind activated by positive action transforms every obstacle into an opportunity, and every delay into destiny."

Ideas Begin To Flow

If you are going to step into the Good Life, you must value the I am Set mindset. When you cross into this realm of ideas, you will begin to experience what is known as Projectional Reasoning. It is the ability to sit in the present and visualize the future. You can sit in 2024 and begin to project yourself into 2030. It's the ability to think ahead, to plan with foresight, and to engage the mind in deliberate forward-thinking. This skill is not just natural, it takes the power of the Holy Spirit coming upon your mind for this to happen because He alone knows the future. With this projectional thinking, even if the future doesn't seem guaranteed, you will realize that it can still be planned because the act of planning will open the door for divine favor, provision, and help, especially when you plan in prayer trusting the Holy Spirit to guide your mind.

When God hasn't explicitly promised you something, this doesn't mean you should remain passive. Rather, it's an invitation to act. Through prayer, strategic thinking, and raising a personal sound– whether through positive declarations, goal-setting, or visualizing the future– you can position yourself in line with divine favor, and position yourself to receive the good things that God has in store for you.

A Motivational Mind

The *I am set* mindset is also a mind that is activated into positive action by receiving positive information. For example, when the Israelites faced the overflowing Jordan River, they could have focused on the obstacle but the overflow of the river didn't deter them because their minds were filled with the blessings of the season. Proverbs 10:22 (KJV) tells us *"The blessing of the Lord, it maketh rich, and he addeth no sorrow with it."* Indeed, when your mind is blessed you will begin to operate at a higher level, where you see the potential in every situation. Unfortunately, those who fail to cultivate their minds fall into the category of individuals who allow *life* to happen to them. Solomon wisely *said "The simple pass on and are punished,"* (Proverbs 22:3 KJV). In modern terms, people who refuse to feed their minds with knowledge and wisdom are setting themselves up for failure. Those who do not seek personal growth and mental stimulation are like ticking time bombs waiting to explode with frustration, anger, and regret.

In relationships, this plays out in interesting ways. For example, if you ask someone about their financial goals such as their credit score, savings plan, or long-term career vision and they respond with anger or defensiveness, it's a sign that their mindset is not prepared for growth. An individual who refuses to embrace self-improvement or plan for their future is not ready for success. This is why, when you are on the path to success and serious about stepping into the good life, you must be intentional about who you partner with, who you relate with and the people you allow into your inner cycle because *He that walketh with wise men shall be wise: but a companion of fools shall be destroyed.* Proverbs 13:20

The *"I Am Set"* mindset asks, *"What have you done to personalize your prophecy?"*, *"What have you done to be better than your last season?"*, *"What have you done to improve who you are?"* If your answer to all this is nothing, then you are not prepared for progress, breakthroughs, and dominion, and you are not prepared for destiny! Life will keep you at your current level and you will never be able to rise! If, for example, you say you will read 30 books in the next two months and you fail to follow through, it's not just a broken promise but a missed opportunity for personal growth."

When You Have This "I Am Set" Mentality, You Become Strong

The *"I Am Set"* mindset doesn't just affect your thoughts; it strengthens your entire being. I know many people are weary, not because their bodies are weak, but because their minds are weak. A weak mind will always lead to a tired soul, but the moment your mind is renewed with fresh information, your soul will be energized, and strength will flow through you. Proverbs 21:22 (KJV) says *"A wise man scaleth the city of the mighty, and casteth down the strength of the confidence thereof."* This scripture shows us the power of wisdom in overcoming obstacles. When you are wise, you will have the ability to pull down any form of resistance because wisdom brings strategy, and strategy brings strength.

The moment you feed your mind with positive, motivational, and forward-thinking ideas, what you are doing is that you are becoming mentally and spiritually fortified to face whatever challenges may lie ahead in your life. Note this: *"A person with a renewed mindset is never easily defeated because they understand that strength is more than physical, it is also mental and spiritual."* Coupled with The *"I Am Set"* mindset gives you the endurance and resilience needed to push through difficult times so that instead of giving in to weariness, you will be able to tap into the strength that comes from having a clear vision and a purpose-driven mind. This is why, in the face of adversity, you must focus on feeding your mind with wisdom and insight, for it is from this place that true strength will emerge, and you will be able to walk [even on water] into your glorious destiny and promised land flowing with milk and honey!

This Mindset Is Transformational

The "I Am Set" mindset is not just motivational; it is transformational because it has the power to change your perception of life and, in doing so, enables you to achieve the results that you desire. When your mind is blessed by God, it becomes a fertile ground for creativity and prosperity. Do you know why? Because you will begin to see opportunities where others see challenges and solutions where others see problems.

This transformation actually begins when you allow your mind to shift from a place of fear and stagnation to a place of hope and progress. It is a mindset that encourages you to constantly envision a better future, even when circumstances seem bleak. Have you ever read Proverbs 23:7 (KJV), *"For as he thinketh in his heart, so is he."* What this means is that your thoughts will be able to shape your reality into a glorious future when you train your mind to think in line with God's promises. So, are you having a bad life? Do you desire something better in life? Then it's time to start thinking in line with God's word.

The first and very important key to this transformation is to realize that there is no problem in life that doesn't have a solution. If you can adopt this mindset, you will no longer be intimidated by challenges. Instead, you will approach every difficulty with the confidence that, with God's guidance, you can find a way through and break into the desired future of Glory. This is why I always caution people to set their minds on God's blessings. When your mind is set on God's blessings, you will have a mental framework that is conducive to success; you will stop settling for losses and you will start envisioning the victories that lie ahead. With this mindset, you don't just survive life's trials, you thrive through them and you begin to experience the abundant life that God promises to those who trust in Him and align their thoughts with His will.

Truly, you must cultivate the *I AM SET* mindset. This is the mindset that God wants you to have because, through this mindset, it is far easier to step into the good life and attain all that He has for you.

CHAPTER EIGHT

WELCOME TO THE GOOD LIFE

"Choosing the good life is not a matter of chance, it's a bold declaration that you will rise above mediocrity and embrace excellence."

You Must Make Up Your Mind And Choose The Good Life

C hoosing the good life is a personal decision that requires intentionality and commitment because it's about deliberately choosing to cross over from mediocrity to excellence, from fear to faith, and from mere survival to living abundantly. The choice you make will determine the life you live. In Deuteronomy 30:19, God places before us the option to choose life or death, blessings or curses. So, can you see that it's up to you to choose– nobody will choose for you? I don't care what you may be going through, you must endeavor to see that the voice of your choice must overpower the voice of doubt, fear, or any other negativity. You must decide to rise above your circumstances, claim your victory, and move forward into the good life that God desires for you. You have toiled enough and now it's time to enjoy the destiny for which you were created.

Choose To Cross Over To The Other Side

Every great journey begins with a decision. So, you must choose to cross over to the other side and be intentional about it! The other side represents your better future, higher calling, and ultimate success. When you make this choice, it's not just a mental decision; it's a commitment to action, a commitment to seriousness, and a commitment to growth both spiritually and physically. It may be stressful, but this is how to choose life and this is how to choose victory over living the *"low life"*. Child of God, you must become determined to succeed, to be strong, and to walk with God better than you may have ever done in the past. Every victory in life begins with a decision to push forward, regardless of the obstacles in front of you. So, make that decision today and right now!

The Power Of Choice

When you look at your life today I want you to realize that everything you see is the outcome of your choices. In other words, *"your ultimate outcomes in life are the product of your choices."* When you choose to trust in God, you generate power through His presence because the more time you spend with Him, the more empowered you become, and the easier life's battles become. You must know that life is not a game of chances; it is a reflection of the choices you make daily, and success in life is the result of your decision to act when God is speaking. *"You must be bold enough to take the steps necessary to achieve your goals today."*

Make Moves, Even If People Don't Understand

There will be moments when people won't understand your decisions, but that shouldn't stop you from moving forward.

God may be calling you to take a step of faith that others can't understand. However, I want you to know that in those moments, you must decide in your heart, *"I will either be the envy of my friends or the most respected among them."* Don't wait for people's approval to move forward; instead, trust in the prophetic guidance of God and go after what He has placed in your heart. *If you have received a green light from God, act on it.*

Take Bold Steps

It's not enough to dream and pray; you must also take bold steps toward your destiny. If God has placed a vision in your heart, then take action today. Go to the car lot and inquire about the car you have been praying for; visit people with the kind of business you have been dreaming of starting; look for the house you desire and ask about the prices. God is saying to you today, *"When the challenges are roaring, it's your harvest season."* Don't let fear or doubt hold you back; just trust in God's timing, and take the leap of faith, knowing that He is with you.

Prepare Yourself For Success

I also want you to know that success doesn't come by chance; it's something you must prepare for. This means that you must learn to spend time talking to God, listening to Him, and seeking counsel from spiritual mentors. You should ask God to open your spiritual eyes and ears so you can discern His will for your life. Also, surround yourself with wise counsel, and people who have been where you want to go and can help guide you. Success is a journey, and you must be equipped with wisdom, faith, and a mindset ready to win. This is how to prepare or you may never be able to step into it!

In life, you will face problems and that's inevitable. However, part of your preparation for success and the key to the good life is learning how to respond to those problems. Instead of complaining, why not be a problem solver? Address the challenges in your life by seeking solutions, and realize that, since you carry the presence of God within you, you are empowered to stand in the middle of danger and still make it to the other side because God has given you the needed strength to overcome! And with His help, no obstacle is too great.

The Prophetic Shortcut To Success

As you walk on this path, I also want you to know that many times, God will provide prophetic shortcuts that will help ease the journey toward success and the good life He has ordained for you faster. But then again, those prophetic shortcuts often come through the long, hard work of the prophets and spiritual leaders who have paved the way. They are the ones who carry the anointing and authority to help guide you into your destiny. So, value and respect the bearers of the Ark; they are the spiritual leaders who carry God's presence and lead you in the right direction. And whether you like it or not, your respect for them will determine the blessings that flow into your life.

Obey And Live The Good Life

Before we finally bring all the revelations that the Lord has been pouring out on this great book to a close, I want to restate this: obedience is one of the greatest keys to living the good life. God has given you instructions, and it's your responsibility to follow them. In truth, He will still give you more in the future too, and sometimes those instructions may look stupid to the human eye, but I want you to know they are designed to lead you into abundance, peace, and fulfillment. *"Obedience is the number one way to come into alignment with God's will, and in that alignment, you will find the good life He has planned for you."*

So, what has He been telling you to do? What steps have you been hesitating to take? I know that obeying God may not always be easy, but I also want you to know it's always the right decision because His instructions are meant to lead you into prosperity, wholeness, and enjoyment, not suffering, bondage, and oppression. With your obedience, you are silencing the negative forces in your life, including sickness, disease, and lack. So, do not trivialize obedience; value it and live by it daily instead!

Just in case you are experiencing pain or struggles, I want you to take a moment to evaluate the source. Is there an area in your life where you are not fully obeying God's instructions? I am asking you to check again because when you choose to follow God wholeheartedly, the pain in your life is meant to dissipate and fade. In your obedience, everything that is not of God must stay on the other side of the river because, through obedience, you cross into a life of joy, peace, and abundance.

Welcome to the good life! A life where you experience prosperity, health, fulfillment, and the fullness of all that God has in store for you! God wants you to live in the fullness of His blessings. So, make the decision today to obey Him in every area of your life, and watch as He leads you into the good life you have been praying for.

CONCLUSION

Many times in life, when challenges become overwhelming, it's easy to wonder, "Does God even care about me?" Many people, even those who firmly believe in God, sometimes fall into the illusion that He is distant or indifferent about their situation, especially when things become really tough. However, nothing could be further from the truth! I want you to know that God's care and love for you are always constant and nothing will ever change it. Also, His deepest desire is to see you live a life filled with joy, peace, love fulfillment, and many wondrous experiences. I tell you the truth and I lie not, God wants you to live the good life, a life overflowing with His blessings.

In Matthew 6:26, Jesus gave us a very comforting reminder of God's love and care by saying *"Look at the birds of the air; they do not sow or reap or store away in barns, and yet your heavenly Father feeds them. Are you not much more valuable than they?"* This is a powerful revelation of God's concern for every aspect of your life. If He takes the time to ensure that the birds are cared for, how much more will He care for you? I want you to know that you are far more precious to Him than anything in nature. God sees every tear you shed, hears every prayer you utter, and understands every worry that weighs on your heart. And because of this, His love is unshakable, and His plans for you are always for your good.

God's care may not always look the way we expect it to look.

Sometimes, when we are going through tough seasons, it can feel like God is silent. But the silence from God is not a sign of abandonment; instead, you need to realize that He is working behind the scenes and preparing all that you will need to experience the glorious life you desire. It is God's ultimate desire that you truly live *the good life*, and I want you to know that He is doing everything to bring you into that life. Even the little things about your life, God cares about it all: He cares about your dreams, your aspirations, and your desires. You can trust Him.

Now that you are done reading through this book, His ultimate desire is that you will put everything you have learned into practice so that you can effectively partner with Him and His plans to bring you into the good life. You may have gained knowledge but don't forget that knowledge alone cannot transform your life. It is not those who hear the words alone who are blessed but those who put them into action.

Now you have heard and so it's time to act, to partner with God, and to cooperate with him so you can step into the Good life and live it in full.

God Bless you!

Welcome to the Good life!

WORKBOOK

Some Questions Vital Questions You Must Answer That Will Guide Your Journey Into The Good Life

Introduction

This workbook is designed to guide you through the principles and revelations that we have taken time to discuss from chapter one through the conclusion of this book. By reflecting on the key messages and completing this exercise, you will be empowered to apply these lessons to your daily life and also step into the good life that God has ordained for you

Chapter 1: The Mystery Of Progress And Divine Guidance

Reflection Questions:

1. Reflect on your definition of progress. How does it align or differ from the concept of "progress" as described in this chapter?

2. Have you ever experienced a situation where something seemed like progress but actually led you away from God? How did you handle it?

Exercise: List three goals you are currently pursuing. For each, assess whether the pursuit is drawing you closer to or further from God. What changes can you make to ensure your progress is in line with divine guidance?

Action Step: Spend 15 minutes each day in prayer or meditation, asking God to reveal areas of your life where you need to refocus on Him.

Chapter 2: Divine Revelations And Your Progress

Reflection Questions:

1. Can you recall a time when following God's direction seemed illogical or difficult? What was the outcome?

2. How do you discern whether a revelation is from God? What steps do you take to confirm His guidance?

Exercise: Write down a recent revelation or insight you believe came from God. How are you acting on it? If you haven't yet acted, outline the steps you will take to do so.

Action Step: Set aside time this week to pray for clarity on any current decisions where God's guidance may seem unclear. Journal what you hear during this time.

Chapter 3: Your Choices Will Guide You To Abundance

"The world's blessings come with sorrow, but God's blessings bring rest and joy."

Reflection Questions:

What choices have you made recently that reflect God's will for your life? How have those choices impacted your peace and joy?

Have there been instances where you chose worldly success over spiritual alignment? What were the results?

Exercise: Reflect on a choice you currently have to make. Compare the potential outcomes of choosing based on worldly wisdom versus divine wisdom. What would God have you do?

Action Step: Memorize Proverbs 10:22 ("The blessing of the Lord makes one rich, and He adds no sorrow with it.") and repeat it daily as a reminder of the importance of God's blessings in your decision-making.

Chapter 4: Moving From Obscurity To Prominence

Reflection Questions:

1. What mindsets or beliefs do you hold that may be limiting your growth and progress?

2. How can you allow God to shape your mindset for greater abundance and success?

Exercise: Write a prayer asking God to reveal any negative mindsets that are holding you back. Afterward, list new, God-centered beliefs you will begin to adopt.

Action Step: Take one action this week that reflects your new mindset of abundance and faith in God's plan for your life.

Chapter 5: The Mystery Of Sounds And Victory In Life

Reflection Questions:

1. How sensitive are you to the sounds and whispers from God? What are some ways you can become more attuned to His voice?

2. Have you ever experienced a breakthrough or victory that was triggered by obedience to a divine instruction? Reflect on this experience.

Exercise: Set aside a quiet moment and ask God to speak to you. After this time, journal any impressions, thoughts, or "sounds" you hear. What steps of obedience are you being led to take?

Action Step: Incorporate daily praise and worship into your routine. Begin each session by intentionally creating a "sound" of victory, trusting that God will move on your behalf.

Chapter 6: Sound Your Way Into Victory Now!

Reflection Questions:

1. What challenges are you currently facing that could be addressed through praise and worship?

2. How can you intentionally use sound (prayer, praise, worship) to create breakthroughs in your life?

Exercise: Choose one area of your life where you need a breakthrough. Dedicate specific times this week to raising a "sound" (through prayer, praise, or declaration) over that area.

Action Step: Commit to praising God daily, even amid challenges. Write down the results and shifts you notice over the next month.

Chapter 7: The Power Of "The I Am Set" Mindset

Reflection Questions:

1. How does your self-identity influence the way you approach challenges and opportunities?

2. What does it mean to fully embrace your identity as a child of God? How can this mindset change your life?

Exercise: Write down the affirmations found in scripture about who you are in Christ (e.g., "I am more than a conqueror," "I am a new creation"). Speak them over yourself each morning.

Action Step: For the next 30 days, consciously reject any negative thoughts about your identity and replace them with the truth of who God says you are.

Conclusion: Stepping Into The Good Life

Reflection Questions:

1. What areas of your life do not yet reflect the "good life" God intends for you?

2. What actions will you take to align more closely with God's plan for joy, abundance, and peace?

Exercise: Take time to write a vision statement for your "good life" based on the principles in this book. Include spiritual, emotional, and practical goals for the next year.

Action Step: Pray over your vision daily, asking God to guide your steps and give you the wisdom to bring His good life into reality.

By completing these exercises and action steps, you are now positioned to experience the full blessings and abundance of the Good Life that God has intended for you. Stay focused, stay prayerful, and trust in God's guidance.

A SPECIAL CALL TO SALVATION & NEW BEGINNINGS FROM APOSTLE DR. DAVID PHILEMON

Dear Beloved,

God loves you deeply and has brought you to this moment for a reason. No matter your past, His love and forgiveness are available to you.

The Bible says in John 3:16, "For God so loved the world that He gave His one and only Son, that whoever believes in Him shall not perish but have eternal life." Jesus Christ came to save you, offering you a new life of purpose and peace.

If you're ready to accept Jesus as your Lord and Savior, pray this simple prayer:

The Salvation Prayer

"Heavenly Father, I come to You in the Name of Jesus. I acknowledge that I am a sinner in need of a Savior. I believe that Jesus Christ is Your Son, that He died for my sins, and that You raised Him from the dead. I repent of my sins and turn to You with my

Whole heart. Jesus, I ask You to come into my life. Be my Lord and my Savior. I surrender my life to You. Fill me with Your Holy Spirit, guide me on the path of righteousness, and help me to follow Your script for my life. Thank you, Father, for saving me. In the name of Jesus. Amen."

Welcome to the Family of God!

If you have just prayed this prayer, Congratulations! You are now a child of God, and heaven is rejoicing. Your journey has begun, and we're here to support you as you grow in faith and discover God's unique plans for you.

Next Steps:

• Connect with a Bible-believing church.

• Read the Bible Daily: God's Word is your guide.

• Pray Regularly: Prayer is your lifeline to God.

• Share Your Faith: Don't keep the good news to yourself.

ABOUT THE BOOK

Are you tired of remaining stuck and on one level? Have you had reasons to cry and wish that life was different? Well, it's time to be welcomed into the good life. God never intended for you to live life just struggling to survive and wishing that things were better. No, not at all. God's ultimate desire is to see you live the Good Life. Picking this book and truly reading it is the missing puzzle as to why you are where you are, and the demands of cooperating with God that will shift you to the next level.

Dear child of God, it is time to read and to get aboard *The Good Life*.

God bless you!

www.ingramcontent.com/pod-product-compliance
Lightning Source LLC
Chambersburg PA
CBHW060345050426
42449CB00011B/2840